HANDBOOKS OF EUROPEAN NATIONAL DANCES

EDITED BY

VIOLET ALFORD

DANCES OF CZECHOSLOVAKIA

Plate 1   Latovák (Vrták step). *Kyjov*

DANCES OF CZECHOSLOVAKIA

MILA LUBINOVÁ

NOVERRE PRESS

**TRANSLATED BY
G. B. SMITH
ILLUSTRATED BY
LUCILE ARMSTRONG
ASSISTANT EDITOR
YVONNE MOYSE**

First published in 1949

This edition published in 2021 by
The Noverre Press
Southwold House
Isington Road
Binsted
Hampshire
GU34 4PH

ISBN 978-1-914311-18-5

© 2021 The Noverre Press

CONTENTS

INTRODUCTION	*Page* 7
Carnival	8
May and Harvest Feasts	9
A Village Wedding	10
Wakes	11
Dances of Ritual Origin	11
Sword Dances	12
Two Regions: East and West	13
Music	14
Costume	16
WHEN DANCING MAY BE SEEN	20
THE DANCES	21
Poise of Body · Time Signatures	22
Basic Steps and Dance Figures	22
Kalamajka (Western form)	27
Kalamajka (Eastern form)	32
Do Kola	34
Latovák	36
BIBLIOGRAPHY	40

Illustrations in Colour, pages 2, 19, 30, 31
Map of Czechoslovakia, page 6

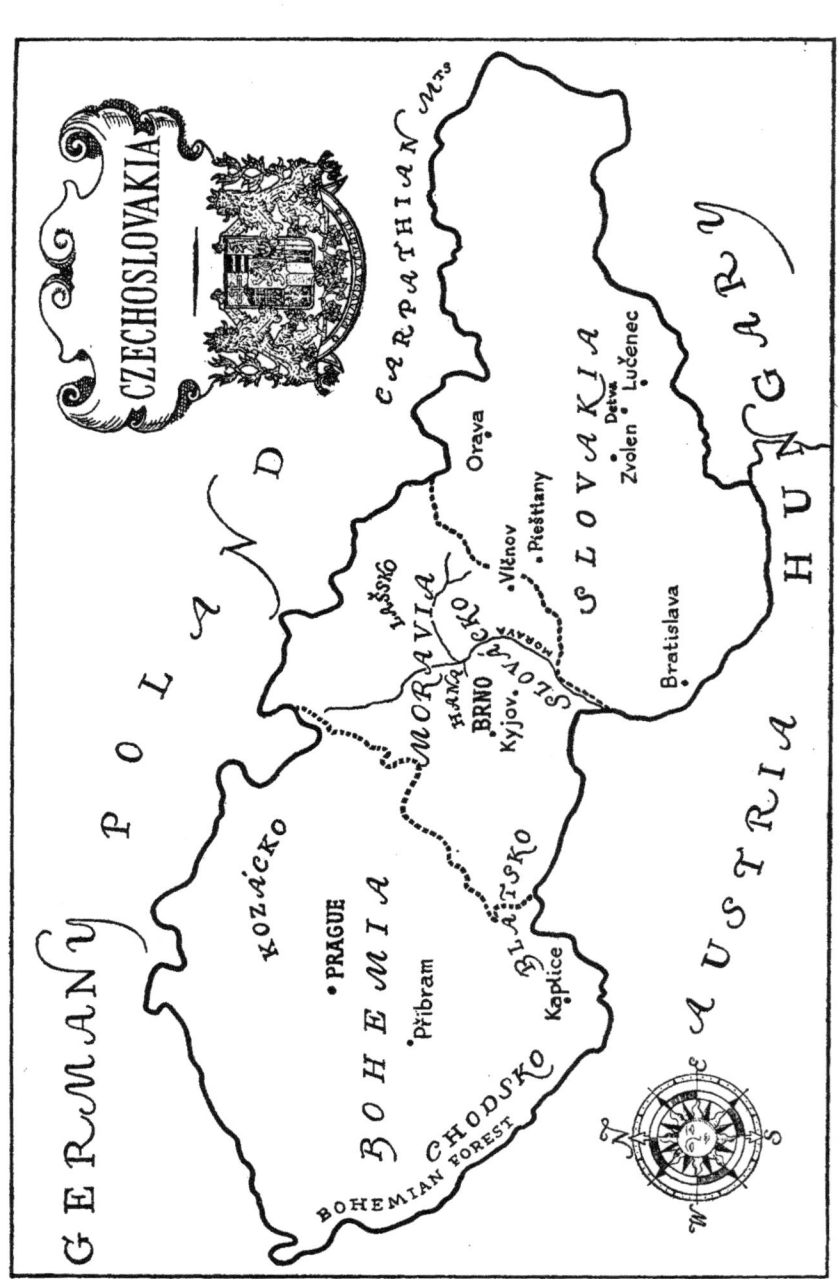

INTRODUCTION

It is an established fact in the history of racial cultures that in the children's games of a nation we see traces of its oldest cultural forms, including those of the dance. The games of Czechoslovak children represent some of the oldest Slavonic dances, since the Czechs belong to a Slavonic tribe which came from a region between the Pripet marshes and the Carpathian mountains, probably in the sixth century. Polish, Russian, and Yugoslav children play many of these same games.

The oldest Slavonic dance did not survive in Czechoslovak lands, although it is still being danced by other Slavonic peoples. According to the evidence this oldest Czechoslovak dance-form is the Closing step (step right foot, close left foot—step left foot, close right foot) in the dance Kotek. This is still preserved as a wedding dance for women, who join hands and dance in a chain through the house, out through the doors and back through the windows. We find the earliest evidence so far of this ancient dance in the sixteenth-century chronicle by Dačický.

Amongst the old children's games is Hela, a singing game, played mostly on Easter Monday and Tuesday, while best-preserved of the old games in dance form is Královničky, The Little Queens, a collection of dance-songs which are still danced by girls on Whit Monday, and sometimes at Eastertime. Nine girls, one of whom is dressed as a queen, go from house to house through the village, dancing and singing until the game—having ensured the coming of Spring—finishes on the green.

These, of all Czechoslovak dances, most resemble the ancient Slavonic dance referred to above, which was itself one of the great family of Circular dances* and was named Kolo or Wheel dance. In chronicles and Church registers we find descriptions of folk dances, even with pictures, the oldest dating from the thirteenth century, and good details can be gleaned from the fifteenth-century writings of Bohuslav Hasištejnský z Lobkovic.

We know that dancing was chiefly performed round the trees on the village green, but that from the fourteenth century special houses were built for it, and some dances have preserved their form well from the sixteenth century. As well as the circular Kotek, mentioned above, there are dances from Silesia, whirling dances such as Hovad, the Gadfly, and chasing dances in which young men and girls pursue each other.

During the sixteenth and seventeenth centuries new dances from Italy came into the Czech lands, for at this time many Italians were invited to the court of the Czech kings, bringing with them Italian culture, which left its mark on Czech Baroque as well as on folk art, and survives still in many dances and songs, as well as in headgear and decorations.

CARNIVAL

Carnival is very gay in Czechoslovakia although it falls, of course, at a time when there is usually hard frost and heavy snow. It begins on 'Fat Thursday' and lasts for nearly a week, till Ash Wednesday.

On Carnival Sunday the village folk gather in the inn for dancing. On the Monday maskers in disguise go from house to house singing and dancing, accompanied by the village musicians. The Tuesday (Shrove Tuesday in England) procession performs a mock ploughing, ploughing up the snow instead of the buried earth beneath it. Sometimes

* See 'Circular Dances' in *Dances of Greece* in this series.

a special Carnival dance is done, Ruchadlo (The Coulter), in which dancers imitate the rocking and bouncing of the plough—true rites of Spring, all unknown to the performers.

Carnival disguises are very different from those of southern countries, but Strakapoun, dressed in ragged attire, reminds us somewhat of the Italian Harlequin. Other favourite disguises are a Devil, a Jew, a Chimney-sweep, a Peasant with his wife and herdsman, Perchta—a horse's wooden head which carries a nosebag full of Carnival pastries—and last but by no means least comes Baba, an old woman who painfully carries a young man in the long carrying basket on her back. In reality it is the young man who carries a dummy of an old woman, head and body down to her waist strapped to his belt in front, giving the illusion of a person bent nearly double. He himself stands through a basket without a bottom, and his legs, with petticoats clinging round them, represent the lower part of the old woman. This is a well-known figure in Central Europe, and here in Czech Carnival the Baba is usually the dancing master of the procession of maskers.

MAY AND HARVEST FEASTS

The next occasion for dancing is the beginning of May. On May Eve every village boy makes a Maypole, and sets it up before dawn outside the house of his chosen girl, while another is for the middle of the village green. On the first Sunday in May the young men go to the inn with music, and afterwards from house to house, inviting the girls for whom they have made their Maypoles to the inn for dancing. Kalamajka and the circular Kolo will be the favourites.

Summer farm work is never-ending, so the next occasion is not until the Harvest festival, and again, later in the autumn, on the Feast of the Dedication of the village church. This usually lasts two days, Sunday and Monday, when there are dances in the inn—often including Zavádky, a Moravian dance proper to the opening of this festal occasion.

A VILLAGE WEDDING

The occasion *par excellence* to enjoy and witness dancing is a village wedding. The celebrations last seven days—none of your afternoon receptions for these wedding guests—and are ordered by a Master and Mistress of Ceremonies, the invitations personally given by the best man and chief bridesmaid. On the evening before the marriage unmarried men and girls prepare crowns of rosemary bound with white ribbons for the girls, and buttonholes for the men. On the wedding morning the best man sallies out with musicians to collect the guests, and with another unmarried man to fetch the bridegroom. These then go together to fetch the bride, the groom and his attendants on horseback, with music of course, singing and firing of pistols. After the Church ceremony the whole party goes to the inn to dance until the wedding meal—at about six o'clock in the evening—is ready at the house of the bride's parents.

Special songs are sung and custom carefully adhered to; dances follow which tell the bride what is before her, for instance Kolíbka, a Cradle: the chief bridesmaid in the centre of the circle, holding a big plate in her arms, as though it were a baby, collects coins from the guests to begin a nest-egg for the expected children. Čepení follows, a lively Ring dance in 3/4 time, the bride placed in the middle. Then comes Plaček, in which the bride's mother hands a large wreath of plaited pastry to the Mistress of Ceremonies, who holds it over her own head dancing three times round the circle, after which it is cut up and a piece given to every guest. It will be noticed that all these dances are of the ancient circular type.

Back at the inn Kotek, another Ring dance, leads off; Korbel, the Beer Jug, follows: bride and groom in the centre drink from a beer jug and take a few turns of a Polka together, each couple following them into the middle.

Midnight sees the procession back at the house of the bride's parents, and serenades go on outside the windows till early morning.

The day after, carts and carriages piled with her new possessions take the bride to her new home in procession, headed by the musicians in the first vehicle playing bagpipes, fiddles and clarinets. Customs are carried out with the greatest respect for tradition, 'buying the bride' with a bridge of coins across the table, a dance *on* the table by the chief bridesmaid, traditional songs proper to the great occasion, and the changing of the girl's green wreath for the matron's kerchief. Three times the bride pulls it off, for she must make a show of unwillingness, but finally the married women prevail, for the new bride must become one of them.

Each day has its own ceremonies, even to the horrid practice of beheading a beribboned cock, so well known in the Pyrenees. In fact the whole cycle of wedding ceremonies conforms exactly to the widespread European tradition, part of which is found in one country, part in another, never the whole in one spot.

WAKES

After the gaiety and perhaps licence of the wedding, we must notice the dancing at the village funeral (as in Spain and Ireland, to mention only two countries), especially on the death of an unmarried person.

DANCES OF RITUAL ORIGIN

Dances which spring from pre-Christian rites can generally be marked, first by their strictly seasonal character, appearing on one day or days of the year only and then disappearing for twelve months, and secondly by their content, which shows something deeper and more purposeful than mere recreation.

There are several variants of a fighting dance with the Valaška as a weapon. This is the traditional long-handled axe, both metal head and wooden handle beautifully hand-decorated with geometrical designs of hammered ornament on the metal, carving or painting on the wood. One such dance is either a man's solo, or a mock fight between two men; another, from the Eastern part of the country, is by a couple, the man twirling and tossing his valaška into the air, his girl partner performing little jumping steps and heel steps. In spite of his strenuous action the man accompanies the movements with a love song. This probably is a ceremonial Courting dance, the man showing off his prowess before his girl. Slovakia possesses a curious Cock Dance, Kohútový Tanec, in which both music and steps imitate a cock strutting and crowing, generally done on the night of the Summer Solstice, June 21st, thus surely showing its ritual origin. Let us briefly name others of this category—Odzemek, a leaping dance similar to the Ukranian Gopak, very probably with the intent to make the corn grow high; Makový Tanec (the Poppy Dance), miming sowing, thinning-out, growth of the poppy plants, picking the flowers and eating the seeds—a mimetic fertility dance like the English 'Oats and Beans and Barley O', which has now come down to the children. There is, too, the seasonal Tug-of-War dance-game, by girls in Orava in the Slovakian Highlands.

SWORD DANCES

More important than any of these is the Sword dance with chain figures, the dancers linked together by the swords held hilt and point, and never let go throughout the many complicated windings. In Germany and Austria this ancient dance was to some degree taken over and kept alive by the guilds, and thus urbanised it became very ornate and stylised. In Czechoslovakia it has remained in its villages and kept a more rustic character, retaining its folk characters, its attendant Fools and Animal-maskers. It flourishes in at least a score of places still, amongst them Kaplice and Příbram, and in the Carpathians and Bohemian Forest. One of those which has been particularly studied is Podšable (Under the Sword), from Podzámčok, a village to the south of Zvolen. They nearly all belong to the very early opening of Spring and therefore to Carnival, often being performed in the snow. A few Sword Dance melodies of the fifteenth century surviving in manuscripts from the Monastery of St. Koruna in Southern Bohemia show us the dance alive in the Middle Ages, and probably little different from what it is now.

TWO REGIONS: EAST AND WEST

To examine the character of Czechoslovak dances it is convenient to divide the country into two regions, Western and Eastern, roughly on the line of the river Morava, showing respectively the influence of Western and Eastern Europe. The Western region is highly developed and industrialised, and folk ways are preserved through tradition without much real life in the soil. The Eastern region is agricultural in the south and pastoral in the north; national costumes are worn in everyday life, folk traditions and customs are alive and still creative. In the Western region folk songs are mostly in the major key, and mostly in the minor in the Eastern region. Four characteristic districts may be given as examples: Chodsko, East Bohemia, Slovácko, and Lašsko.

In Chodsko the national costume shows strong Renaissance influence. The songs are coloured by the local dialect which is richly rhythmical and musical. The people are handsome, fine physical specimens, and have always been freemen, without feudal domination. Skill and endurance are marked characteristics of their dancing, and they have finely developed mimetic dances.

In East Bohemia the people tend to be intellectually gifted in respect to music and dancing. Their rhythms are not overwhelming, nor, as in Slovakia and Slovácko, primitive and springing from the soil, but aesthetically they are highly developed.

The dances of Slovácko and Lašsko are a real treasury of dance motifs. Rhythmically they are very rich, yet as disciplined as those from East Bohemia, full of life and as fascinating as those of Slovakia, having at the same time more dynamic elements.

MUSIC

The oldest record of musical instruments and songs accompanying Slav dances is a mural painting of the eleventh century in the Slavonic church in Kiev (Ukraine), showing musicians and dancers such as lived in Czechoslovakia at the same period. The oldest musical instruments referred to in Czechoslovak chronicles are the Kobza, a lyre-like instrument, the viol and the Lučec (hurdy-gurdy or vielle), also pipes and drums.

Village bands were composed chiefly of bagpipes in Southern Bohemia, of violins and bagpipes in other parts. In Eastern Bohemia music is more developed, and bands contain violins, clarinets and double basses, and in some parts also horns and trumpets.

The character of the dance-songs was much influenced by these typical instruments, for folk music in the Western region used modulations into the dominant (major) and in Slovakia tended to modulate to the sub-dominant (minor). The modulation to the dominant shows the influence of the bagpipes, which in this country are only capable of major keys, and is the most marked characteristic of the music of the Western part of the land.

The dulcimer (cymbalon), which is the typical instrument in South-East Moravia and Slovakia, has a string for every tone and semitone, and the possibilities of modulation with this instrument into any key have influenced the melodic and harmonic development of the music of those parts. The typical Slovakian folk band was composed of a dulcimer and one or two violins, and this arrangement has had a special influence on dance form.

Gypsy Musicians. The musicians are usually gypsies whose playing has an extraordinary flexibility in tempo. As a result of this the Čardáš, which is usually solely connected with Hungary, is the best-known dance throughout Slovakia, in spite of the fact that until about a hundred years ago the bagpipes were commonly used in these parts. The mountain shepherds accompany their songs and dances on an enormous pipe somewhat like a rustic bassoon, called Fujara.

Dance-Songs. Since so many dances are performed to sung music a word on this subject may be of interest here. To begin with, the names of dance-songs derive from a characteristic step, from the pattern of the dance, from the districts where they are popular, or from the mime. Sometimes a purely instrumental interpolation at beginning, middle or end occurs, to lengthen the music when the dance is longer than the song used for it. Sometimes dancing and singing alternate to an'instrumental accompaniment, the singer being usually the man of the couple.

Czechoslovak Dances classified. The great majority are Pair dances, a few are Figure dances such as the old Quadrille. These come into the Recreational category. The Ritual category we have already dealt with. Musically and choreographically they can be classified under the following headings:
1. Those with one tempo, although figures and steps may change. Example: Kalamajka.
2. Those with changes of tempo. Examples: the Slovakian Čardáš and most of the Slovakian dances.
3. Those in which the change of tempo and measure divides the dance into two or more sections. Examples: Rejdovák and Rejdovačka.

4. A special group in which the measure changes but the tempo does not. To form a choreographical phrase, two measures may be combined—for instance three bars of 2/4 followed by one bar of 3/4—the value of the crotchet remaining the same, and the steps are arranged to fit exactly. This group is found only in the Western part of the country. Example: Salát.
5. There is also the Furiant rhythm, the natural 2/4 measure being converted into two 3/4 bars containing three 2/4 bars, i.e. six beats. The music for this type is chiefly of instrumental origin.

COSTUME

In the *Western regions* national costume has disappeared from everyday life except in a few villages, and a late influence is apparent in the costumes that have survived. The oldest forms in these regions are in East Bohemia. The following can be taken as examples—Blatsko and Kozácko, called after the districts where they are found. In both a big shawl about two yards square goes over the bonnet and round the neck. It is white with open embroidery in Kozácko, and in Blatsko white, embroidered with brightly coloured bead-work from one corner over nearly half of it. In Kozácko the skirt is white over a pink silk petticoat, in Blatsko it is of woollen material in darkish colours with a band of silk brocade. At both places the bodice is of dark velvet, the stockings of knitted red cotton, the shoes plain black and low-heeled. The men have yellow leather breeches; long coat and waistcoat of dark blue with brass buttons in Blatsko; in Kozácko the waistcoat black, the coat dark green, and a brightly coloured scarf is worn at the neck.

In *Moravia* the costumes are the richest and most beautiful in the country, and it is here one sees the men in long tight white woollen trousers, with felt boots reaching half-way up the calf. Women like white for weekday skirts, with a black knitted sash wound tightly round them and tied behind. On Sundays they wear saffron skirts and yellow-embroidered aprons. The embroidery shows its Byzantine origins in geometric motifs, and, except on bodice and yellow Sunday apron, is always white. Their headkerchiefs are of painted linen, but on Sundays a long band of linen is tied behind the head with two richly embroidered ends hanging down the back. Married women wear a bonnet beneath the kerchief. In winter both men and women put on their sheepskin coats with the fleece inside, the skin outside embroidered in colours.

In *Slovakia*, costume divides itself into that of the rich lowlands and that of the poorer highlands. The lowlands show tight trousers and high riding boots, embroidered sleeves and a loose white coat. For women the skirt reaches only to the knees and is of coloured serge, flowered voile or dark-blue printed linen, worn over many, many petticoats—sixteen is not unknown. For festive occasions this short skirt is white, and it is here we find the embroidered boots similar to those of the men. In winter a short sheepskin or fur-trimmed coat hides their finery. The same type of costume goes all over Slovakia, but each district has its own colouring. In South Slovakia a strong Hungarian influence is apparent; towards the South-East a Balkan type creeps in, especially at Zvolen and Lučenec.

Among those which should be worn for the dances here given we find a couple from two places in Slovakia, the woman from Pieštiany, the man from Detva, performing a step of Do Kola (Plate 2a). The man's white-fringed breeches and black embroidered apron, embroidered bolero-like waistcoat and the curious shape of his sleeves should be noted. The girl's magnificent embroideries, great puffed sleeves and curious headdress, which can be covered by a white kerchief tied under her chin, are set off by the strong colour of her skirt.

The second picture on Plate 2 shows a couple from the Chodsko district in Western Bohemia performing the Holubička (Dove) step in the Western version of the Kalamajka. The man's white-backed waistcoat has a blue front with yellow embroidery; embroideries on the frontsides of his breeches come down in points. Note the embroidered strip at the back of his breeches and the great red tassels on his top-boots. The girl's dress is characterised by immense puffed sleeves, a lovely lace apron and a black embroidered head-scarf. The skirt is stiffly pleated.

The Eastern Kalamajka (Plates 3 and 4) is danced by a couple from Vlčnov, Eastern Moravia. The girl's costume is one of the best-known, with its great concertina sleeves, red tassels, edged sash and top-boots. Her partner is equally magnificent with embroideries on trousers and short waistcoat, wrists and shoulders, and tassels on the waistcoat. A feather sets off his cap.

Plate 1 shows another well-known costume, that of Kyjov, the girl with black embroidery on her white blouse and collar, and magnificent coloured work on her apron sash ribbons, bonnet and bodice. The man has equally good designs on trouser-fronts, bolero, shirtfront and wrists. He wears artificial flowers and a swaggering feather on his small black hat. They are dancing the Vrták (Drill) step in Latovák from West Moravia.

One cannot find that these varied costumes have influenced the dances to any noticeable extent. They all allow ample freedom to the limbs and lend themselves beautifully to dance movements. Rather do costume and dance together show those characteristics inherent in the life of particular districts, as for example at Haná in the flat lands of Central Moravia, where agriculture is prosperous. There dances are grave and stately, costume of rich materials. In South Moravia, where there are vineyards and orchards, the dance is very lively and in quick *tempo*, while the costume is very gay and brightly coloured.

Plate 2

Do Kola. Detva (man), Piešťany (woman)

Kalamajka (Western version). Chodsko

SEASONS AND OCCASIONS WHEN DANCING MAY BE SEEN

Carnival   In Czechoslovakia this season begins on 'Fat Thursday', the Thursday before Lent, and lasts till Ash Wednesday; especially lively on Shrove Tuesday.

Easter Monday and Tuesday   Children's seasonal dance-games.

Whit Monday (sometimes Easter)   Královničky (Little Queens).

First Sunday in May

Harvest Feasts

Village Patronal Feasts   Always postponed till autumn on account of agricultural work.

Weddings   Celebrations last seven days.

Funeral Wakes

Village Fairs   Dates must be ascertained on the spot.

THE DANCES

TECHNICAL EDITOR, MURIEL WEBSTER
ASSISTED BY KATHLEEN P. TUCK

ABBREVIATIONS
USED IN DESCRIPTION OF STEPS AND DANCES

r—right ⎰ referring to R—right ⎰ describing turns or
l—left ⎱ hand, foot, etc. L—left ⎱ ground pattern
C—clockwise C-C—counter-clockwise

For descriptions of foot positions and explanations of any ballet terms the following books are suggested for reference:

A Primer of Classical Ballet (Cecchetti method). Cyril Beaumont.

First Steps (R.A.D.). Ruth French and Felix Demery.

The Ballet Lover's Pocket Book. Kay Ambrose.

REFERENCE BOOKS FOR DESCRIPTION OF FIGURES:

The Scottish Country Dance Society's Publications. Many volumes, from Thornhill, Cairnmuir Road, Edinburgh 12.

The English Folk Dance and Song Society's Publications. Cecil Sharp House, 2 Regent's Park Road, London N.W.1.

The Country Dance Book I–VI. Cecil J. Sharp. Novello & Co., London.

POISE OF BODY · TIME SIGNATURES

The dances are for the most part gay and the carriage is upright and sometimes proud, especially that of the men.

The 4/4 tempo is used only in the oldest Czechoslovakian dances, some of which survive in the Eastern region but only a few in the West. Even March steps are usually in 2/4 or 3/4 tempo. The most usual time-signatures are 2/4, 3/4 and 3/8, while 5/4 is occasionally found.

BASIC STEPS AND DANCE FIGURES

Sousedska (Neighbour's Song). This step is used in the dance of the same name and also in Latovák, combined with other steps. It is usually danced in 3/4 time. It resembles a Waltz step and may be danced forward, sideways or turning.

	MUSIC *Beats*
BASIC STEP:	
Step forward or sideways on r foot.	1
Slide l foot to r, raising the heels.	2
Step forward or sideways on r foot (very short step).	3
Repeat, beginning with the l foot.	
This basic form is usually reserved for older people.	
VARIATIONS:	
A Step sideways on r foot.	1–2
Close l foot to r foot.	3
This variation is often used at the end of a dance figure.	
B Step forward or sideways on r foot.	1
Close l foot with a stamp.	2
Step forward or sideways on r foot (very short step).	3

c Step forward on r foot. ‖ 1
  Hop on r twice. ‖ 2–3
  The hops are very small and the feet scarcely leave the ground.

The above basic step and variations can be used in the following ways:

DANCE FIGURES:
1. In twos, man on R of woman with inside hands joined. Couples start with inside feet and turn alternately face to face and back to back, travelling forward.
2. In twos with Waltz grasp. The couple revolves on the spot or turns progressing forward.
3. The woman turns with hands on hips in front of the man, who travels forward with no turn. He has one hand on his hip and with the other hand turns the woman by her elbows.

Obkročák. This step is used in a dance of the same name, and in Latovák combined with other steps. It is danced in 2/4 tempo, one step to each bar, or sometimes in 3/4, one step to each bar.

	MUSIC *Beats*
BASIC STEP:	
Step forward on r foot.	1
Turn on the ball of r foot, turning to R.	2
Repeat on l, still turning to R.	1 & 2

VARIATIONS AND DANCE FIGURES:

A In twos, man on R of partner, his l arm round her shoulders and her r arm round his waist, other hands linked in front. The dancers move on a small circle about a point in front of them, turning half-way round to each bar. Man begins on l foot, woman on r. The movement of the variation is:

> Spring on l foot.
> Hop on l foot.
> Repeat with spring and hop on r.

Both spring and hop are very low.

B As in A but in double time, two steps to each bar.

C As in A but with much bigger spring and hop. Very accented.

D Grasp as in A. Step on l. Hop twice on l. Repeat on r.

E Grasp as in A. Stamp on l. Beaten hop on l. Repeat on r.

F This variation is called *Vrták* (step revolving like a drill) and was at one time forbidden as being too wild. The grasp is closer than in A and the step takes two bars (see Latovak):

> Spring on l foot, hop on l foot .. .. 1 bar
> Big hop on l foot, hop on l foot .. .. 1 bar
> Repeat, beginning on r foot.

The largest amount of turn is performed on the 1st beat of the 2nd bar.

G As Vrták, only much smoother. This variation was introduced to the ballroom in 1884 under the name of *Polka Tremblante*.

H As in the basic step but with an exaggerated sway from side to side.

N.B.—In all the variations the free leg may be beaten against the calf of the other leg during the hopping movements (pas battu).

Polka. When this step appeared in Czechoslovakia in the early part of the nineteenth century it supplanted the Obkročák. The step appears to have originated in Czechoslovakia and was developed in Eastern Bohemia (but Poland claims it also). This step is danced in 2/4 tempo.

	MUSIC
BASIC STEP: Quickly.	*Beats*
Step on r foot.	1
Close l to r, lifting r leg quickly forward.	&
Step on r foot.	2
The step can be danced in any direction—forward, sideways, backward and turning.	

VARIATION (Stamped Polka):
As in basic step, but marking each beat with a stamp.

Holubička (The Dove). This step is used in Sivá Holubička or Sekerečka and in Kalamajka (Western form). It can be danced in either 2/4 or 3/4 tempo, as it is simply a running step with one step to each beat.

DANCE FIGURE:
Partners face each other, r arms linked and l hands on hips. They run in C direction for two bars, change arms and run C-C for two bars.

Přitukdvaný (Rapped Step). This step is used in the Eastern or Moravian forms of Kalamajka. It is danced in 2/4 or 4/8 tempo and has two forms, a slow and a quick.

BASIC STEP AND DANCE FIGURES:	MUSIC
A Slow.	*Beats*
Step on r foot, leaving l leg out to side; hold for 2 and 3.	1 2 3
Close l to r, clicking the heels together and bending both knees.	4
The whole step is then repeated on l foot.	
The above step is used in the following way: Partners stand opposite one another, both hands on hips, and both begin with r foot so that they move away from one another. Repeat on l foot, partners moving towards one another.	

B Quick.
   Hop on r foot, clicking heels together in the air. Repeat three times on r foot.
        and 1
        & 2 & 3
        & 4

In this form partners stand facing one another with r hands joined and l hands on hips. They turn half-way round C on the four hopping steps. Both dancers hop on r foot when r hands are joined and on l foot when l hands are joined.

Točinky (Turning Step). It is danced in 4/8 tempo—'andante'—as in Do Kola.

BASIC STEP:
   Step sideways on r, turning half-turn to R.
   Step sideways on l, to complete the turn to R.
   Repeat this alternately on r and l feet, moving and turning to R for eight beats, i.e. two bars.
   Partners travel away from one another to sides of the room and may repeat the step towards one another. Hands are held on hips.

Přísunný. This step is used in Do Kola in 4/8 time (two steps to a bar).

BASIC STEP AND DANCE FIGURE:
   Step to side on r foot.   1
   Close l to r, bending both knees slightly.   2
   Repeat to L.   3 4
   This step, in which the movements are very light and gentle, is used in the following way:—Partners face one another with Waltz grasp, man on the R. He starts with r foot while the woman starts with l foot.

VARIATION AND DANCE FIGURE:
   As in the basic step, but the 2nd and 4th beats are accented by clicking heels together.

The whole expression of the variation is one of tension and the step is hard.

It is used in the following way:—Partners stand facing one another, hands on hips, not too close, and gradually move closer, so that the direction of each step is side and slightly forward.

Otáčivý (Turn). This step is used in Sedlácká and in Slovakian wedding dances. It is danced in 2/4 time.

BASIC STEP:

Step forward on r foot.	1
Swing l foot forward, turning to R on r foot.	and
Close l foot to r foot.	2

Repeat, always stepping forward on r foot with a continuous turn to the R.

DANCE FIGURE:

Partners face each other, holding as for the Waltz, man turning on his r foot as described and woman doing the same step on l foot.

KALAMAJKA (*Western form*)

Region	(This dance has two forms, Western and Eastern.) Western form. Costumes from the Chodsko region, Western Bohemia. Plate 2(b).
Character	Simple.
Formation	Couple dance. Partners start facing one another, about three yards apart, with hands on hips.

Dance	MUSIC
Both start on r foot.	*Bars*
	A
1 Hop twice on r foot, swinging l leg forward and backward.	1
One stamped Polka forward on l foot.	2
Hop on l foot, swinging r leg forward and backward.	3
One stamped Polka forward on r foot.	4
Repeat above on r and l feet.	5–8
N.B.—The Polka movement is danced almost on the spot.	
2 *Holubička step*	B
8 runs linking r arms with partner to make two whole turns.	9–12
8 runs linking l arms with partner to make two whole turns in the opposite direction.	13–16
Repeat the whole dance.	

KALAMAJKA (Western form)

From the Western region
Arranged by Arnold Foster

Intro. March tempo

A *Dance*

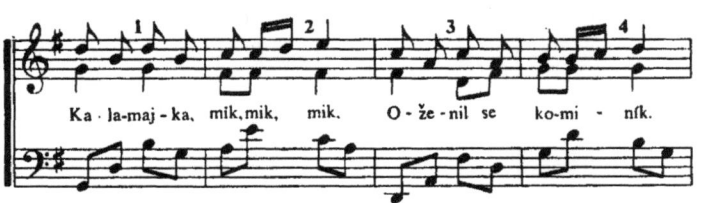

B

Plates 3 and 4   Kalamajka

(Eastern version). Vlčnov

KALAMAJKA (*Eastern form*)

Region	Eastern. Costumes from Vlčnov, Eastern Moravia. Plates 3 and 4.
Character	Quick and vigorous.
Formation	As in Western version. Hands are on hips.

Dance
Man begins on l, woman on r foot.

	MUSIC Bars
	A
1 2 Polka steps forward.	1–2
4 Přitukávaný steps (quick version), man hopping 4 times on r foot, woman on l foot.	3–4
Repeat Polka and Přitukávaný steps.	5–8
During this figure the couple turns to the man's L, the woman travelling C-C and the man remaining on the inside of the circle throughout.	
Repeat all this, making another whole circle to the man's L.	1–8
2 The couple now dances C round the room, inside hands grasped, man on R of woman.	**B**
Step forward on inside foot with a stamp; close outside foot to inside foot.	9
Step forward again on inside foot with a stamp, turning slightly away from partner and swinging the outside leg forward.	10
Repeat this step on outside foot, turning slightly towards partner, then on inside and outside feet alternately, eight times in all.	11–24
Repeat the whole dance as often as desired.	

KALAMAJKA (Eastern form)

From the Eastern region
Arranged by Arnold Foster

DO KOLA

Region	Eastern. Woman's costume from Pieštiany (western Slovakia), man's from Detva (central Slovakia). Plate 2(a).
Character	The dance works up from a quiet soft movement to one of strong tension.
Formation	Couple dance. Partners face each other, arms round each other's waists, free hands clasped in front. Men on outside of circle.

Dance	MUSIC Bars
1 6 Přísunný steps (man begins on r foot, woman on l foot).	1–3
2 Hands on hips: 8 Točinky steps, both starting with the r foot, and turning away from one another to the R to either side of the room.	4–5
8 Točinky steps back towards one another, to finish facing partner but not too close.	6–7
3 The Variation of the Přísunný step (man on r, woman on l foot), partners gradually moving towards one another with hands on hips, ready to repeat the whole dance.	8–10

DO KOLA

From the Eastern region
Arranged by Arnold Foster

Andante

The dance works up from a quiet soft movement to one of strong tension.

LATOVÁK

Region	Western. Costumes from Kyjov, western Moravia. Plate 1.
Character	The charm of the dance lies in the unexpected rhythm, the music being written in both 2/4 and 3/4 time.
Music	The dance consists of two rhythmic phrases (denoted by *a* and *b*, which must not be mistaken for the usual A and B of the music):

$a = $ 1 bar of 3/4, 2 bars of 2/4;
$b = $ 3 bars of 2/4, 2 bars of 3/4.

The phrases are arranged in this pattern:
a a b / a a b / b b / a a b

Formation	The couples dance C round the room, holding as described in Obkročák (Variation A), and turn continuously to the R. The men start on the outside of circle.

Dance

	MUSIC Bars
a One Sousedska step turning half to R (man on l foot, woman on r foot).	1
One Vrták step (Variation F of Obkročák) turning once and a half to R. (N.B.—Half a turn is easier to perform, but loses the character of the step.)	2–3
a Repeat *a*.	4–6
b Three Obkročák steps (Variation A) making half a turn to the R on each step.	7–9
Two Sousedska steps turning to finish with the men on the inside of the circle.	10–11

a a b	Repeat the above steps. Couples finish with men on the outside of the circle.	12–22
b	Three Obkročák steps, two Sousedska steps turning as before.	23–27
b	Repeat *b* to finish with men on the outside of the circle.	23–27
a a b	Dance *a a b* as in bars 1–11, but do not repeat, so that couples finish the dance with the men on the inside of the circle.	28–38

Repeat the whole dance as often as desired.

LATOVAK

From the Western region
Arranged by Arnold Foster

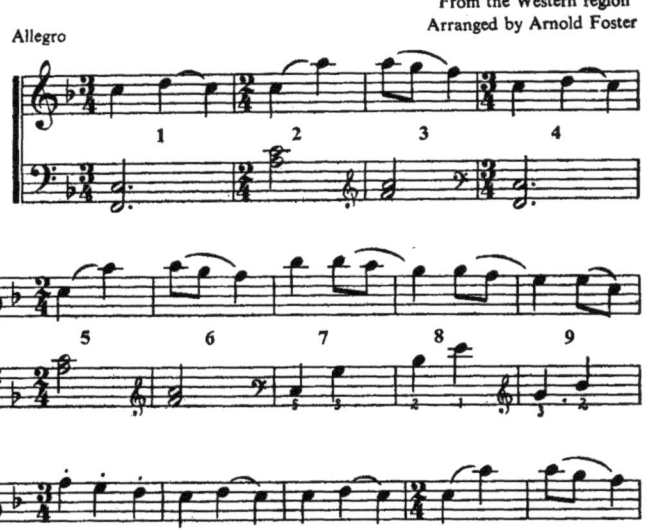

Summary of Steps in Latovák

a	1 Waltz step, spring hop hop hop (Vrták)	1–3
a	,, ,, ,, ,, ,, ,, ,, ,,	4–6
b	3 Spring hops (Obkročák), 2 Waltz steps	7–11
a	1 Waltz step, spring hop hop hop	12–14
a	,, ,, ,, ,, ,, ,, ,,	15–17
b	3 Spring hops, 2 Waltz steps	18–22
b	,, ,, ,, ,, ,, ,,	23–27
b	,, ,, ,, ,, ,, ,,	23–27
a	1 Waltz step, spring hop hop hop	28–30
a	,, ,, ,, ,, ,, ,, ,,	31–33
b	3 Spring hops, 2 Waltz steps	34–38

Note.—Throughout the dance the position of the feet is similar to that used in an old-fashioned Waltz, where first the woman then the man steps between partner's feet on the first beat of each bar.

NOTE

Traditional costumes are the treasured heritage of the people to whom they belong. Those of Czechoslovakia are renowned for embroidery designs, different in every village and handed down from one generation to another. Any attempt to reproduce these intricate costumes should be gone about with the greatest care and respect. They are not fancy dresses, therefore there should be nothing fancy about them.

The Editor

BIBLIOGRAPHY

CHOTEK, V.—*Lidová kultura a kroje v Československu.* (National culture and costumes in Czechoslovakia.) Prague, 1937.

ERBEN, K. J.—*Prostonárodní české písně a říkadla.* 1862–64. (Czech folk songs and nursery rhymes.)

JANÁČEK, L.—*Národní tance na Moravě.* 1891–93. (National dances in Moravia.)

NĚMCOVÁ, B.—*Obrazy z okolí domažlického.* 1845. (Essays from the Domažlice country.)

SEIDEL, J., and ŠPIČÁK, J.—*Zahrajte mi do kola.* Prague, 1943. ('Play me a dance tune.')

SUŠIL, F.—*Moravské národní písně s nápěvy do textu vřaděnými.* 1860. (Moravian national songs, with tunes.)

VELINSKÝ, B.—*Czech, Moravian and Slovak Dances.* (Music and Notes separately.) Ling Physical Education Association's Publications.

VYCPÁLEK, J.—*České tance.* (Czech dances.)

VYDRA, J.—*Nauka o kroji.* 1931. (Study of Folk Costumes.)

WOLFRAM, RICHARD.—*Schwerttanz und Männerbund.* Vol. II. Kassel, 1936–38. (Sword-dance and men's societies.)

ZÍBRT, C.—*Jak se kdy v Čechách tancovalo.* 1895. ('As they used to dance in Bohemia.')

ZICH, O.—*České lidové tance s proměnlivým taktem.* From *Revue d'Ethnographie Tchécoslovaque.* (Czech folk dances with changing rhythm.)

Film: PLICKA, K.—*Zem spieva.* (The earth sings.) Obtainable from the Ministry of Information, Valdštejnská 10, Prague III.

These titles have been translated to help English readers who may not be able to read the text but would profit by studying the music, dance-figures and illustrations.

www.ingramcontent.com/pod-product-compliance
Lightning Source LLC
Chambersburg PA
CBHW061743290426
43661CB00127B/965